KETO DIET FOR BEGINNERS AND PROS

How to Lose Weight with Quick and Healthy Keto Diet
Recipes - Bonus: 45 Days Weight Loss Challenge

1st Edition

ISBN- [9781074918156]

The author's ideas and opinions contained in this publication serve to educate the reader in a helpful and informative manner. We accept the instructions may not suit every reader and we expect the recipes not to gel with everyone. The book is to be used responsibly and at your own risk. The provided information in no way guarantees correctness, completion, or quality. Always check with your medical practitioner should you be unsure whether to follow a low carb eating plan. Complete elimination of all misinformation or misprints is not possible. Human error is not a myth!

DISCLAIMER

What Is The Keto Diet?

Keto diet is a shortened term for "ketogenic" diet. It refers to the focus on burning ketones instead of glucose. Ketones are the result of fat production while glucose and insulin are the result of carbs. Such diet mainly comprises of food items which are rich in fat. An ideal keto diet item should include 70-80% fat in it.

This diet is also often named as a low carb diet since the amount of carbohydrate in keto dishes is significantly low. Typically, the item has around 5% carb. Combining these two terms together, one may also call it LCHF or Low Carb High Fat diet.

How Does A Keto Diet Work?

High portions of carbohydrates help your body produce large amounts of glucose and insulin. The body can use glucose to prepare energy in the easiest way. As a result, it uses these glucose molecules primarily to create energy. When your body has too much glucose, the fats it ingests remain unused. This way the amount of stored fats increases which can then result in higher health risks.

When you reduce the amount of carbohydrates, the body instantiates a process called ketosis. During this process, ketones are formed to breakdown the fats stored in the liver. The body then switches to burning ketones as their primary source of energy. This is the state we try to achieve through a keto diet plan. Since starving someone of food entirely is not a wise chose, keto diet helps to remove the excess carbohydrates.

How Does A Keto Diet Help In Building Muscles?

It is a common misconception where people equate the intake of carbohydrates to muscle building. You can achieve the same muscular build and strength with a keto diet. The only thing you have to make sure, other than performing regular exercises, is the inclusion of high protein. To get a rough idea of how high this amount of protein intake should be, calculate how much lean pound of body mass you have. You must have 1 gram of protein for each pound.

There are mainly three types of ketogenic diets. We discuss each of them below:

STANDARD KETOGENIC DIET

This is the normal keto diet most people follow. It has no special requirement and simply focuses on fatty food items. Anyone can follow this version of keto diets.

CYCLICAL KETOGENIC DIET

The cyclical ketogenic diet or CKD is specially targeted at the body-builders. They follow the keto diet on a weekly basis. That means, they dedicate one day per week to take large amounts of carbohydrates so that their glycogen stores are not exhausted. Then they go back to the keto diet.

TARGETED KETOGENIC DIET

On a targeted ketogenic diet or TKD, one eats a little bit of fast-digesting carbs so that they have enough energy before hitting the gym. This is meant for the general health-conscious people who like to work out on a regular basis.

Due to the long practice of breaking down carbohydrates, your body may have much fewer enzymes to deal with fats. So during the initial phase of a keto diet, it still uses the remaining portion of glucose to produce energy. This may make you feel a lot less energetic for the first week. You may suffer from headaches, cramps and dizziness during this time period since the electrolytes are getting out of your body. Some simple ways to tackle this is to eat sodium-rich (salty) food and drink a lot of water. Sodium helps to replenish the lost electrolytes.

After this transition period is over, your body will get used to the keto diet and then function normally again. Give it a few days and your body will start burning ketones just as promised.

Advantages of a Keto Diet

The benefits of keto diet are not limited to diabetic solutions. There are a lot more advantages of switching to a low-carb diet, as we have discussed below:

BLOOD SUGAR UNDER CONTROL

Keto diet is incredibly helpful for patients who are suffering from diabetic conditions. Besides, it can also help others to stay away from this disease. Compared to low-calorie diets, ketogenic diets offer a much safer path in diabetes prevention.

The root cause of diabetes is high levels of blood sugar which causes disruption in the insulin function. This, in turn, triggers a noticeable change in the metabolism of your body. According to a 2005 study conducted by the Ann Intern Medical, a keto diet can enhance the insulin sensitivity of your body by 75%. Another study showed that switching to a keto diet can help type-2 diabetic patients to get rid of the medications altogether.

With this diet, your body can remove the excess fat which triggers type-2 diabetes. It is a natural way to decrease blood sugar levels and keep them under control at all times. Our hormone insulin enhances its effectiveness by preventing sugar cells to cause more problems. It grows weaker with the increasing amount of carbohydrates and sugary foods. A keto diet can help us achieve a stronger immunity against diabetes by lowering the blood sugar level significantly.

WEIGHT LOSS

Since the body switches to fats as the primary energy source, the keto diet reduces your weight effectively. Multiple pieces of research have proved that this diet works better than the popular low-fat diet. One of the best aspects of losing weight this way is that you don't have to limit your calorie intake. You can still allow yourself to enjoy delicious food items like chicken roasts, casserole, pizza and other similar dishes.

Contrary to the low-fat diet, the keto diet includes a larger amount of daily protein intake. Protein is known to keep your appetite filled more than the other macronutrients and thus your hunger levels lower naturally.

BETTER FOCUS

Have a greater mental focus with the help of keto diets. Since the keto diet avoids triggering huge spikes in blood sugar, your brain automatically can perform better at concentration. A neuroprotective antioxidant like ketone has the power to stop dangerous reactive oxygen species from harming your brain cells.

It also helps the ageing brain cells to maintain their health. As a result, your mental health will stay in its ideal state for a longer time if you go on a keto diet. You can avoid neurological disorders like Parkinson's and Alzheimer's by following this diet.

INCREASED ENERGY

There is a limitation to how much glycogen your body can store. As a result, in any other diet full of carbs, your body has to constantly draw in glycogen from various sources to keep its energy level up. On the keto diet, this is not an issue. That is because the main energy source of your body on a keto diet is the fat. Unlike glycogen, you can store as much fat as you want in the body. You will never run out of energy sources this way. So you can feel healthier and energetic no matter what time of the day it is.

NO SATIATION

Unlike the typical diets, this one does not force you to live on leafy vegetables and lean meats. You don't feel the curse of being starved throughout the day. Keto diets are more sustainable since it allows the inclusion of delicious recipes. All you have to ensure is that they are cooked the right way and with the right balance of ingredients. Since you eat moderate amounts of heavy food on a regular basis, you feel more satiated and this state persists for a longer time.

EPILEPSY TREATMENT

Those who have been suffering from epilepsy can give the keto diet a shot. Before it became a lifestyle changer, it was used in the 1900s for epilepsy treatment. A considerable majority of epilepsy patients consists of children. Dr Russel Wilder of Mayo Clinic designed this diet in 1924 to treat epilepsy in children which proved to be very effective.

Epilepsy is basically a nervous system disorder which triggers seizures. Since keto diets have a strong impact on improving brain functions, it can help the patients bring epilepsy under control. It is especially useful for those children who have been unresponsive to anti-epileptic drugs.

IMPROVING CHOLESTEROL LEVELS

It may occur to you that the high levels of fat on a keto diet can hamper your cholesterol levels. However, the reality could not be further from it.

Fats are molecules which repel water (which is why oil or grease never mixes with water). Triglycerides and cholesterol are two kinds of fats. The first one helps to store energy and the second one does multiple maintenance functions for the body.

The HDL cholesterol or high-density lipoproteins are the good cholesterol which your body should get more of. By switching to a keto diet which restricts your daily carb intake within 50g, you can increase the HDL portions and have better control on your cardiovascular health.

IMPROVING BLOOD PRESSURE CONDITIONS

Blood pressure or BP is the force that the blood vessels feel from the blood travelling through them. Its standard measure is 120/80 mm Hg as declared by the American Heart Association. The people with a diastolic BP (the denominator) of 80-90 mm Hg suffer from hypertension. This condition can lead to severe diseases like stroke, myocardial infarction and even death if not taken care of early.

A diet consisting of large portions of healthy fats can combat against such hypertension. The Journal of American Medicine published a study in 2007 which showed the effectiveness of keto diet in lowering hypertension. Each subject had a drop in their blood pressure by 7.6 mm Hg on average.

INSULIN RESISTANCE

Insulin resistance can cause type 2 diabetes very easily. Insulin itself is a hormone secreted by the pancreas which maintains the metabolism of carbohydrates and fats. It breaks down these materials into glucose molecules so that the body cells can manufacture energy from them. It also maintains a standard level of glucose in blood. Insulin resistance occurs when the body cells stop reacting to the hormone as a result of imbalanced levels of glucose in the bloodstream. Keto diet can pose a solution to this issue by improving insulin sensitivity. A 2005 study showed a whopping 75% increase in this sensitivity among its type-2 diabetic patients.

REDUCING ACNE

If you are suffering from skin diseases like acne, a low-carb diet like keto can help by lowering skin inflammation. High portions of carb can trigger acne. So by reducing daily carb intake and following skin cleaning routines, you can easily get rid of the acne spots.

Encouraged to eat:

UNPROCESSED MEATS

Meats are often looked upon as demons in many diets. However, the realit is, unprocessed meats are extremely helpful for maintaining health. Such meats are comparatively low in carbohydrates and high in protein. But since the focus of a keto diet is high portions of fat instead of protein, try to keep the meat intake to a minimum. Otherwise, your body will utilize all that extra protein to prepare glucose preventing you to enter the ketosis phase.

So add poultry, lamb and pork belly to your diet dishes. Avoid processed meats like meatballs and sausages. If you like a new meaty product, make sure its ingredients have carbohydrates under 5%.

FATTY FISH

Fishes which are high in oil or fat can be a great addition to keto diets. Salmon, tuna, trout, herring and mackerel get your body the necessary omega-3 fatty acids. These fats are great for your cardiovascular health and help you live a long life. They also have high portions of vitamin B and potassium. The people struggling to lose weight can depend on them to increase insulin sensitivity and decrease insulin levels.

SEAFOOD

In addition to fishes, other kinds of seafood are also rich in essential fats. Shellfishes like shrimp, squids, octopus, oysters, clams and mussels include an incredibly low level of carbohydrates. Their carb counts swing only between 3 to 7 grams per serving. Be sure to include at least 2 dishes prepared with these every week.

EGGS

Eggs are helpful in almost every diet scenario. Especially in a low-carb diet, it can be very useful since there are so many ways to cook an egg. One of these contains about 6 grams of protein and less than a gram of carbohydrates. As a result, you will see it very frequently in our keto diet recipes. Eggs also help you feel fuller and thus lower your hunger levels.

Many people prefer leaving the egg yolk. But in fact, it also contains a large number of nutrients. Specifically, the antioxidants like zeaxanthin and lutein help to keep your eyes in a healthy condition. Even though they have high cholesterol levels, eggs in fact help with cardiovascular health by modifying LDL shape.

VEGETABLES

Low-carb vegetables which grow above the ground are ideal choices for a keto diet. Broccoli, cauliflower, cabbage, asparagus, tomatoes and zucchini have the most frequent appearances among keto diet dishes. One way to enhance their taste and get good fat at the same time is to cook these veggies in butter. You can also drizzle lots of olive oil on a veggie salad. Use these vegetables to replace your cravings for rice, pasta and potatoes.

HIGH-FAT DAIRY

This is the most exciting part of keto diet for many food-lovers. Can you imagine being away from cheesy pizza and casseroles for months? We certainly can't. This low-carb diet helps you get creative with your love for high-fat dairy elements like cheese, yogurts, heavy cream and butter. However, avoid including milk in a keto diet meal. Also, don't have "low-fat" yogurts since they include high amounts of sugar.

NUTS

You may add a moderate amount of nuts to your keto dishes. It is also a popular form of snacks. However, don't get carried away while eating them as snacks since it is very easy to lose track of how much you have already taken. If possible, avoid cashews altogether since they have high carbs. Pecan nuts, almonds, walnuts and macadamia nuts are much better options.

AVOCADO

Avocados have always been a great choice for dietary habits. We highly recommend it for keto diets as well due to its incredibly low carb portions. Half of a regular avocado includes only 2g of net carb. These also have high portions of vitamins and minerals. It is rich in potassium which makes the transition period of a keto diet much easier.

HEALTHY OILS

Olive oil and coconut oil will allow you to fry ingredients in a healthy way. The first one has high portions of oleic acid which prevents heart disease. Its extra-virgin version reduces inflammation and enhances artery function. Since it has no carbs, olive oil is often used for salad dressings in keto diet items.

Coconut oil, on the other hand, has MCTs which are easy for the liver to absorb and transform into ketones. Patients of Alzheimer's disease have used coconut oil in the past to raise their ketone levels. It is also helpful for people to lose weight, especially belly fat.

BERRIES

Fruits are almost forbidden for a keto diet. However, berries do no harm. You can add a few strawberries, raspberries and blackberries to a delicious dessert item. Especially pairing them up with whipping cream will make the dish much more delectable.

Discouraged to eat:

SUGAR AND SUGARY FOODS

Strictly stay away from sugary beverages like soft drinks, sport drinks, fruit juice and vitamin water. The usual ready-made sugary foods like candy, chocolate bars, donuts, cookies and cakes must also be thrown out of your dietary habits. While purchasing a new product, check its label for any artificial sweetener. It is also highly recommended to keep the use of honey, agave and maple syrup at bay.

STARCHES

Rice, bread, pasta and potatoes are pretty much the staple food in many countries. However, all these have to go out of the window when you begin a keto diet. In our recipes, we have included one for keto bread so that you can prepare your own version of the delicious bread which will not compromise your ketogenic aspirations. Avoid other forms of starch like legumes, whole grain products and some of the root vegetables as well.

MOST FRUITS

The majority of fruits include too much sugar. You can have one per week at most, but taking them daily will do no good to your keto diet.

DIET PRODUCTS

Even though these products are marketed as essential items for a weight-loss regime, they are actually highly processed and contain high amounts of carbohydrates.

ALCOHOL

Did you know beer is basically liquid bread? It is almost entirely made of absorbed carbohydrates. If you can find a low-carb beer, maybe go for it instead. Otherwise, hands off the beers.

GIVE YOUR REFRIGERATOR A MAKEOVER

Before going out and buying loads of keto foods, you need to clean out your refrigerator of the other food items you have stored so far. Go through each rack and drawer. Take out the items you are strictly prohibited from. You may leave some of the less harmful ones to take later in moderation. Donate this food to the people in need if possible. It's always the little things which matter.

STOCK UP THE KETO FOODS

Now that you have made room in the refrigerator for new keto foods, buy the ones you need and stock up. Instead of the starches and sugary carbs, bring in more ketogenic staple food items like fatty meats, avocado, butter and coconut oil. For more food suggestions, take a look above and go through the most frequently used ingredients.

READ SOME BOOKS

There are many good books available on ketogenic diets which go into details of the food items, recipes and nutrition. Buy or rent a few of them and enlighten yourself. Make sure the writer is credible though. Doctors, dieticians and scientists make the best of these books. Some of the keto books we recommend are "Keto Clarity", "The Art and Science of Low Carb Living" and "The New Atkins for a New You".

EAT BEFORE SHOPPING

Never go shopping on an empty stomach. You may end up buying way too many items you were not even planning on purchasing. We understand the cravings for sweets, cakes and chocolates but you must obey your ketogenic values first. So have a small meal of good healthy fatty ingredients before going into the groceries.

DRINK LOADS OF WATER

No matter what diet you are following, staying hydrated is a must. Drink 8 glasses of water at minimum everyday. One way to figure out how much water you need to eat on a daily basis, first divide your total body weight (measured in pounds) by 2. Then divide this result by 8. The result is the number of glasses of water you must drink per day.

BREAKFAST

Time: 35 minutes | Serves 4

Net carbs: 3% (4g/0.14oz) | Fiber: 0.3% (1g/0.03oz) | Fat: 88% (48g/1.7oz)

Protein: 9% (11g/0.4oz) | Kcal: 498

INGREDIENTS:

- ◆ 5 oz bacon
- ◆ 4 oz cream cheese
- ◆ 2 oz lettuce
- ◆ 3 eggs
- ◆ 1 sliced tomato
- ◆ 4 tbsp homemade mayonnaise

- ◆ ½ tsp baking powder
- ◆ ½ tbsp psyllium husk powder
- ◆ A pinch of salt
- ◆ ¼ tsp tartar cream
- ◆ Fresh basil

PREPARATION:

1. Whisk the egg whites with salt and tartar cream until it gets stiff.

2. Separately, mix egg yolks, cream cheese, psyllium husk powder and baking powder.

3. Fold the first mixture into this yolk mixture.

4. Bake the cloud bread pieces in batches of 4 until they turn golden.

5. Cook the bacon until crispy.

6. Spread 1 tbsp of mayonnaise on each cloud bread piece. Top it with bacon and the vegetables in layers.

Time:7 minutes | Serves 1

Net carbs: 0% (0g/0oz) | Fiber: 0% (0g/0oz) | Fat: 99% (38g/1.3oz)

Protein: 1% (1g/0.03oz) | Kcal: 330

INGREDIENTS:

- ◆ 1 cup freshly brewed coffee
- ◆ 1 tbsp coconut oil
- ◆ 2 tbsp unsalted butter

PREPARATION:

1. Blend all the ingredients until you receive the texture you want for your coffee. Serve hot and fresh!

Time: 20 minutes | Serves 4

Net carbs: 4% (5g/0.2oz) | Fiber: 2% (3g/0.1oz) | Fat: 82% (39g/1.4oz)

Protein: 11% (13g/0.5oz) | Kcal: 420

INGREDIENTS:

- ♦ 1 cup whipping cream
- ♦ ½ cup berries (blueberries, strawberries, raspberries etc.)
- ♦ 7 oz cottage cheese
- ♦ 2 oz coconut oil
- ♦ 4 eggs
- ♦ 1 tbsp psyllium husk powder

PREPARATION:

1. Mix eggs, cheese and psyllium husk powder. Leave it for a few minutes.

2. Cook the pancakes at medium-low heat in a non-stick skillet heated with coconut oil.

3. Whip up the cream separately and serve the fresh pancakes with them. Top with a few berries you love.

Time:15 minutes | Serves 4

Net carbs: 2% (1g/0.03oz) | Fiber: 0% (0g/0oz) | Fat: 70% (22g/0.8oz)

Protein: 28% (15g/0.5oz) | Kcal: 272

INGREDIENTS:

- ♦ 5 oz sliced bacon
- ♦ 8 eggs
- ♦ Parsley and cherry tomatoes for topping

PREPARATION:

1. Fry the bacon slices until they turn crisp and transfer to a bowl.

2. Cook the eggs in the same pan.

3. Serve them both with cherry tomatoes and parsley.

Time:17 minutes | Serves 4

Net carbs: 2% (4g/0.14oz) | Fiber: 0.5% (1g/0.03oz) | Fat: 75% (43g/1.5oz)

Protein: 22% (25g/0.9oz) | Kcal: 510

INGREDIENTS:

- 1 oz butter
- 1 oz shredded cheese
- 3 eggs
- 3 mushrooms
- ⅛ yellow onion
- Salt
- pepper

PREPARATION:

1. Whisk the three eggs with salt and pepper.

2. Heat up the frying pan with melting butter and add in the whisked mixture.

3. Spread the cheese, onion and mushrooms when the egg is still a bit raw.

Time: 5 minutes | Serves 1

Net carbs: 8% (10g/0.35oz) | Fiber: 1% (1g/0.03oz) | Fat: 85% (43g/1.5oz)

Protein: 6% (4g/0.14oz) | Kcal: 415

INGREDIENTS:

- ◆ 7 oz coconut milk
- ◆ ½ tbsp lemon juice
- ◆ ¼ cup blueberries
- ◆ ¼ tsp vanilla extract

PREPARATION:

1. Blend in all the ingredients until it reaches a smooth texture. Taste and serve!

Time: 12 minutes | Serves 2

Net carbs: 3% (4g/0.14oz) | Fiber: 4% (5g/0,.18oz) | Fat: 84% (49g/1.8oz)

Protein: 9% (9g/0.3oz) | Kcal: 486

INGREDIENTS:

- ◆ 2 eggs
- ◆ 2 oz butter
- ◆ 8 tbsp coconut cream
- ◆ 1½ tbsp coconut flour
- ◆ Pinches of salt and ground psyllium husk powder

PREPARATION:

1. Mix in the ingredients and cook on a non-stick saucepan at low heat. Stir until the texture satisfies you.

2. Serve fresh with coconut cream and some berries.

Time:1 hour 5 minutes | Serves 2

Net carbs: 2% (3g/0.1oz) | Fiber: 3% (4g/0.14oz) | Fat: 70% (55g/1.8oz)

Protein: 25% (41g/1.45oz) | Kcal: 678

INGREDIENTS:

- 7 eggs
- 14 oz pumpkin puree
- 3 oz smoked salmon
- 2¼ oz butter
- 1 oz leafy greens
- 1¼ cups almond flour
- 1¼ cups coconut flour
- 1/3 cup unsweetened apple sauce
- ⅓ cup flaxseed
- ⅓ cup pumpkin seeds
- ⅓ cup chopped walnuts
- ¼ cup coconut oil
- 2 tbsp pumpkin pie spice
- 2 tbsp heavy whipping cream
- 1 2/3 tbsp psyllium husk powder
- 1 tbsp baking powder
- 1¼ tsp salt
- A pinch of chilli flakes

PREPARATION:

1. Grease the bread pan with oil or butter.

2. Mix in the dry ingredients.

3. In a separate bowl, mix pumpkin puree, egg, oil and apple sauce. Then add this mixture to the previous dry mixture for preparing a smooth batter.

4. Bake them on the lower rack with some pumpkin seeds on top for an hour.

Time:32 minutes | Serves 2

Net carbs: 10% (16g/0.6oz) | Fiber: 6% (10g/0.35oz) | Fat: 75% (51g/1.8oz)

Protein: 10% (16g/0.6oz) | Kcal: 610

INGREDIENTS:

- ◆ 1 avocado
- ◆ 4 eggs
- ◆ 2 diced tomatoes
- ◆ 4 minced garlic cloves
- ◆ 1 chopped orange bell pepper

- ◆ 2 minced jalapenos
- ◆ 1 chopped yellow onion
- ◆ 4 tbsp coconut oil
- ◆ Cilantro

PREPARATION:

1. Heat 2 tbsp coconut oil. Saute the onion, bell pepper, jalapeno and garlic until they have become soft.

2. Then add in the tomatoes and saute for a few more minutes.

3. Heat up the rest of coconut oil in another non-stick skillet. Cook the eggs at medium-low heat for 5 minutes.

4. Top the eggs with salsa, cilantro and avocado slices before serving.

Time: 15 minutes | Serves 4

Net carbs: 2% (2g/0.07oz) | Fiber: 1% (1g/0.03oz) | Fat: 70% (18g/0.6oz)

Protein: 27% (14g/0.5oz) | Kcal: 230

INGREDIENTS:

- ◆ 3 oz shredded cheese
- ◆ 6 eggs
- ◆ 1 finely chopped tomato
- ◆ 1 finely chopped scallion
- ◆ 2 finely chopped pickled jalapenos
- ◆ 2 tbsp butter
- ◆ Pinch of salt and pepper

PREPARATION:

1. Fry the scallions, tomatoes and jalapenos in butter for 2 minutes.

2. Add whisked eggs to it and scramble.

3. Add salt, cheese and pepper at last. Serve fresh!

Time: 21 minutes | Serves 8
Net carbs: 33% (4g/0.14oz) | Fiber: 16% (2g/0.07oz) | Fat: 33% (4g/0.14oz)
Protein: 16% (2g/0.07oz) | Kcal: 60

INGREDIENTS:

- 4 chopped medium zucchini
- 2 finely chopped large tomatoes
- 2 tbsp olive oil
- 1 finely chopped medium onion
- ½ tsp pepper
- 1 tsp salt

PREPARATION:

1. Heat up a large skillet with some oil at medium-high heat. Cook the onions there until they get tender. Add zucchini to it and stir.

2. Add salt, pepper and tomatoes for about 5 minutes. Serve with spoon.

Time: 22 minutes | Serves 12

Net carbs: 50% (5g/0.18oz) | Fiber: 20% (2g/0.07oz) | Fat: 20% (2g/0.07oz)

Protein: 10% (1g/0.03oz) | Kcal: 50

INGREDIENTS:

- 1.5 lbs thinly sliced carrots
- 1.5 lbs thinly sliced radishes
- ¼ cup chopped cilantro
- 6 chopped green onions
- 2 tbsp extra virgin olive oil
- 3 tbsp orange juice
- 3 tbsp lemon juice
- 1 tsp orange zest
- 1½ tsp lemon zest
- ½ tsp salt
- ¼ tsp pepper

PREPARATION:

1. Mix carrots, radishes, cilantro and onions.

2. Blend the other ingredients for dressing.

3. Toss the salad with dressing and refrigerate for an hour.

Time: 26 minutes | Serves 6

Net carbs: 0.6% (2g/0.07oz) | Fiber: 0.3% (1g/0.03oz) | Fat: 26% (9g/0.3oz)

Protein: 65% (22g/0.8oz) |

Kcal: 192

INGREDIENTS:

- 1.5 lbs ground beef
- 1 finely chopped onion
- 1 minced garlic
- 2 tbsp minced mint
- 3 tbsp minced parsley
- ¾ tsp pepper
- ¾ tsp ground allspice
- ½ tsp ground cinnamon ½tsp salt
- ¼ ground nutmeg
- Lettuce leaves for serving

PREPARATION:

1. Combine all ingredients in a bowl except beef.

2. Add the beef and mix well. Carve them into 6 oblong patties.

3. Grill each patty at medium heat or up to 160-degrees.

4. Serve each pattie on a lettuce.

Time: 32 minutes | Serves 6

Net carbs: 16% (6g/0.2oz) | Fiber: 11% (4g/0.14oz) | Fat: 25% (9g/0.3oz)

Protein: 47% (17g/0.6oz) | Kcal: 186

INGREDIENTS:

- 1 lbs lean ground beef
- 14.5 oz reduced-sodium beef broth
- 12 oz chopped green chillies
- 1 chopped onion
- 6 cups chopped cabbage
- 1 tbsp olive oil
- 2cups water
- ¾ tspgarlic powder
- 2 tbsp minced cilantro
- ½ tsp salt
- ¼ tsp pepper

PREPARATION:

1. Cook the beef with seasonings and crumble it at medium-high heat.

2. After taking out the beef, heat the pan with oil. Then saute cabbage and onion there for 5 minutes.

3. Add the beef, broth, chiles and water. When it starts boiling, reduce the heat and let it cook for 10 minutes.

4. Stir cilantro in the end and serve fresh.

Time: 30 minutes | Serves 16

Net carbs: 29% (5g/0.18oz) | Fiber: 18% (3g/0.1oz) | Fat: 29% (5g/0.18oz)

Protein: 24% (4g/0.14oz) | Kcal: 81

INGREDIENTS:

- 3 lbs trimmed brussel sprouts
- 5.3 oz crumbled goat cheese
- ¼ cup olive oil
- 8 minced garlic cloves
- 1 tsp salt
- ½ tsp pepper

PREPARATION:

1. Preheat the oven to 420-degrees.

2. Mix all ingredients other than cheese.

3. Roast the mixture in oven for about 25 minutes.

4. Toss and serve with cheese.

Time: 34 minutes | Serves 6

Net carbs: 21% (10g/0.35oz) | Fiber: 0% (0g/0oz) | Fat: 34% (16g/0.6oz)

Protein: 45% (21g/0.7oz) | Kcal: 270

INGREDIENTS:

- ◆ 6 7-oz boneless chicken breast halves
- ◆ 1-1/8 cup bread crumbs
- ◆ ½ cup grated Parmesan cheese

- ◆ 2 tsp Dijon mustard
- ◆ ½ cup melted butter
- ◆ 1 tsp Worcestershire sauce
- ◆ Pinch of salt

PREPARATION:

1. Preheat the oven to 345-degrees.

2. Mix the sauce, butter, mustard and salt.

3. Spread bread crumbs and cheese in a separate bowl.

4. Dip each chicken piece in the butter mix first and pat it in the crumbs.

5. Bake the pieces uncovered until their temperature reaches 165-degrees.

Time: 25 minutes | Serves 4

Net carbs: 4% (12g/0.4oz) | Fiber: 2% (5g/0.18oz) | Fat: 75% (112g/4oz)

Protein: 19% (48g/1.8oz) | Kcal: 1260

INGREDIENTS:

- 25 oz shredded green cabbage
- 24 oz chorizo
- 1½ cups heavy whipping cream

- 2 oz + 2 tbsp butter
- ½ cup chopped parsley
- Salt and pepper
- Zest of half a lemon

PREPARATION:

1. Cook the chorizo in butter at medium heat on a skillet. Transfer them to a bowl.

2. Saute the shredded cabbage on the same skillet until golden brown. Add the cream.

3. When it starts boiling, lower the heat and leave simmering until amount of cream has gone down.

4. Add salt, pepper, parsley and lemon zest while serving with the chorizo.

Time: 5 minutes | Serves 2

Net carbs: 5% (3g/0.1oz) | Fiber: 14% (8g/0.3oz) | Fat: 62% (34g/1.2oz)

Protein: 18% (10g/0.35oz) | Kcal: 374

INGREDIENTS:

- ◆ 4 oz lettuce
- ◆ 2 oz sliced edam cheese
- ◆ 1 oz butter
- ◆ 2 sliced cherry tomatoes
- ◆ 1 sliced avocado

PREPARATION:

1. Spread butter on lettuce leaves.

2. Add remaining ingredients as toppings and serve.

Time: 15 minutes | Serves 4

Net carbs: 5% (2g/0.07oz) | Fiber: 0% (0g/0oz) | Fat: 21% (8g/0.3oz)

Protein: 74% (28g/1oz) | Kcal: 191

INGREDIENTS:

- 4 5-oz tilapia fillets
- 2 tbsp reduced-fat mayonnaise
- ¼ cup grated Parmesan cheese
- 1 tbsp softened butter
- 1 tbsp lime juice
- ¼ tsp salt
- ⅛ tsp pepper
- ⅛ tsp garlic powder
- ⅛ tsp dried basil
- Pinch of onion powder

PREPARATION:

1. Mix all ingredients except fillets and salt.

2. Coat a foiled baking pan with cooking spray, put the fillets and spread some salt.

3. Broil them 3 inches from heat.

4. Sprinkle the first mixture over them and broil again for 2 minutes.

Time:31 minutes | Serves 4

Net carbs: 33% (5g/0.18oz) | Fiber: 21% (3g/0.1oz) | Fat: 33% (5g/0.18oz)

Protein: 13% (2g/0.07oz) | Kcal: 90

INGREDIENTS:

- ◆ 6 oz sliced asparagus
- ◆ 2 julienned sweet red peppers
- ◆ 2 halved and sliced yellow summer squashes
- ◆ 8 tbsp white wine
- ◆ 5 tsp olive oil
- ◆ Pinch of salt and pepper

PREPARATION:

1. Saute the vegetables in a skillet with oil and wine. You can add any in-season vegetable instead of the listed ones.

2. Add the seasonings and serve.

Time:55 minutes | Serves 6

Net carbs: 6% (7g/0.3oz) | Fiber: 3% (2g/0.07oz) | Fat: 55% (60g/2oz)

Protein: 36% (39g/1.4oz) | Kcal: 739

INGREDIENTS:

- 2 lbs skinless, boneless chicken thighs cut into bit-sized pieces
- 1 lb chopped cauliflower
- 7 oz shredded cheese
- 4 oz cherry tomatoes (halved)
- 1 finely chopped leek
- ¾ cup sour cream
- ½ cup cream cheese
- 2 tbsp butter
- 3 tbsp green pesto
- Juice of half a lemon
- Salt and pepper

PREPARATION:

1. Preheat the oven to 200-degrees Centigrade.

2. Melt butter to fry the chicken with seasonings of salt and pepper.

3. Mix the cream, pesto, cream, salt, lemon juice and pepper in a different bowl.

4. Put the fried chicken pieces on a greased baking dish and top it with cream.

5. Add the pieces of cauliflower, leek, cherry tomatoes and cheese as toppings too.

6. Bake for half an hour.

Time: 25 minutes | Serves 4

Net carbs: 6% (7g/0.3oz) | Fiber: 0% (0g/0oz) | Fat: 57% (67g/2.4oz)

Protein: 37% (43g/1.5oz) | Kcal: 793

INGREDIENTS:

- 20 oz turkey breast
- 7 oz cream cheese
- 2 cups heavy whipping cream
- ⅓ cup small capers
- 1 tbsp tamari soy sauce
- 2 tbsp butter
- Salt and pepper

PREPARATION:

1. Preheat the oven to 175-degrees Centigrade.

2. Melt 1 tbsp butter in an ovenproof frying pan.

3. Season the turkey and then fry it until a golden brown color is formed.

4. Transfer the pan into oven and let it reach a temperature of 74-degrees Centigrade. Then transfer it to a plate and foil.

5. Separate the turkey drippings. Add the cheese and cream to it. Stir them till they start boiling lightly. Let it simmer and get thicker.

6. Season with salt and pepper.

7. Saute the capers with remaining butter until they turn crispy.

8. Serve the turkey with fried capers and sauce.

Time: 20 minutes | Serves 6

Net carbs:17 % (3g/0.1oz) | Fiber: 11% (2g/0.07oz) | Fat: 50% (9g/0.3oz)

Protein: 22% (4g/0.14oz) | Kcal: 112

INGREDIENTS:

- 6 cups of finely shredded cauliflower
- ½ cup grated Asiago cheese
- 2 tbsp unsalted butter
- 1 tsp garlic-herb seasoning
- 1 tbsp extra virgin olive oil

PREPARATION:

1. Heat oil, butter and seasoning in a skillet.

2. Add the cauliflower slowly and cook for a few minutes.

3. Stir the cheese into the concoction and serve.

Time: 30 minutes | Serves 4

Net carbs: 11% (6g/0.2oz) | Fiber: 2% (1g/0.03oz) | Fat: 29% (16g/0.6oz)

Protein: 58% (32g/1.2oz) | Kcal: 325

INGREDIENTS:

- 1¼ lbs beef top sirloin steak
- ½ lb sliced assorted mushrooms
- 1 sliced leek
- 1 cup dry red wine
- 2 tbsp olive oil
- 1-2/3 tbspCajun seasoning
- 1 tsp minced garlic
- 1 tbsp butter
- ¼ tsp pepper
- Pinch of salt

PREPARATION:

1. Season the steak with Cajun seasoning and leave it be for a few minutes.

2. Cook it in oil for a while until the temperature gets up to 135-145 degrees.

3. After removing the steak, saute leek and mushrooms in butter.

4. Add garlic to this concoction and keep cooking for one minute.

5. Mix in wine, salt and pepper.

6. When it starts to boil, keep it cooking until the liquid level decreases by 50%.

7. Slice up the steak and serve with the mushroom sauce.

Time:22 minutes | Serves 4
Net carbs: 11% (4g/0.14oz) | Fiber: 5% (2g/0.07oz) | Fat: 27% (10g/0.35oz)
Protein: 57% (21g/0.7oz) | Kcal: 201

INGREDIENTS:

- ◆ 1 lb uncooked, peeled and deveined shrimp
- ◆ 1 cup halved cherry tomatoes
- ◆ 8 cups baby spinach
- ◆ ¼ cup sliced and toasted almonds
- ◆ 3 minced garlic cloves
- ◆ 2 tbsp chopped parsley
- ◆ 2 tbsp butter
- ◆ Some lemon halves
- ◆ Pinch of salt and pepper

PREPARATION:

1. Take a large skillet and melt butter on it at medium heat. Saute shrimp and garlic there for 3 minutes. Add parsley to the mixture.

2. Arrange tomatoes and spinach on the serving plate. Top them with the shrimp mixture. Add salt, pepper, lemon juice and almonds on it.

Time: 30 minutes | Serves 4

Net carbs: 11% (6g/0.2oz) | Fiber: 3% (2g/0.07oz) | Fat: 16% (9g/0.3oz)

Protein: 70% (39g/1.38oz) | Kcal: 274

INGREDIENTS:

- ◆ 4 6-oz skinless boneless chicken breast halves
- ◆ 1 cup milk
- ◆ 4 cups broccoli florets
- ◆ 1 tbsp all-purpose flour
- ◆ 1 cup chicken broth
- ◆ 1 tbsp snipped fresh dill
- ◆ 1 tbsp olive oil
- ◆ ½ tsp garlic salt
- ◆ ¼ tsp pepper

PREPARATION:

1. Season the chicken with pepper and garlic salt. Then cook it at medium heat until it turns brown.

2. After taking out the chicken, cook broth and broccoli in it. When they reach a boiling temperature, simmer for 5 minutes. Take out the broccoli after it gets tender.

3. Mix dill, flour and milk in another bowl. Slowly stir this mixture into the broth and cook until it gets thick.

4. Add the chicken and cook until its temperature reaches 165-degrees. Serve it with broccoli.

Time: 30 minutes | Serves 4

Net carbs: 2% (5g/0.18oz) | Fiber: 1% (1g/0.03oz) | Fat: 76% (90g/3oz)

Protein: 21% (53g/1.8oz) | Kcal: 1043

INGREDIENTS:

- ♦ 8 eggs
- ♦ 12 oz shredded mozzarella cheese
- ♦ 10 oz shredded cheese (any type you prefer)
- ♦ 4 oz leafy greens
- ♦ 3 oz pepperoni

- ♦ 8 tbsp olive oil
- ♦ 6 tbsp unsweetened tomato sauce
- ♦ 2 tsp dried oregano
- ♦ Seal salt
- ♦ Black pepper

PREPARATION:

1. Preheat the oven to 200-degree Centigrade.

2. Prepare the crust by whisking the eggs and stirring shredded mozzarella to it. Spread this batter on a baking sheet in the shape of two circles or one rectangle. Bake for 17 minutes.

3. Raise the oven's temperature to 225-degree Centigrade.

4. Add the fillings of pizza with a layer of tomato sauce, some oregano, a cheese layer and then pepperoni.

5. Bake it again until the color has turned golden brown.

6. Serve the freshly baked pizza with fresh salad.

Time: 15 minutes | Serves 2

Net carbs: 4% (7g/0.3oz) | Fiber: 9% (14g/0.5oz) | Fat: 60% (96g/3.5oz)

Protein: 27% (43g/1.5oz) | Kcal: 1100

INGREDIENTS:

- 4 eggs
- 2 avocados
- 12 oz canned crab meat
- ½ cup mayonnaise
- 1½ oz baby spinach
- ½ cup cottage cheese
- ½ tsp chili flakes
- 2 tbsp olive oil
- Salt and pepper

PREPARATION:

1. Boil the eggs first soft or hard, according to your preference. Peel them.

2. Arrange crab meat, avocado, spinach, mayonnaise, cottage cheese and the egg on a plate.

3. Season the spinach a little with salt, pepper and olive oil. Add some chili flakes to the avocado and serve.

Time: 30 minutes | Serves 4

Net carbs: 7% (9g/0.3oz) | Fiber: 4% (5g/0.18oz) | Fat: 57% (75g/2.6oz)

Protein: 32% (42g/1.5oz) | Kcal: 880

INGREDIENTS:

- 25 oz salmon
- 15 oz cauliflower
- 14 oz coconut cream
- ½ cup chopped cilantro
- 1 oz olive oil
- 4 tbsp butter
- 2 tbsp red curry paste
- Salt and pepper

PREPARATION:

1. Preheat the oven to 200-degrees Centigrade.

2. Arrange the fish pieces on a greased baking dish. Season each piece with salt and pepper. Put 1 tbsp butter on each piece.

3. Combine curry paste, coconut cream and cilantro. Spread this mixture on fish.

4. Bake for 21 minutes in the oven.

5. Boil the florets of cauliflower in slightly salted water for 2 minutes.

6. Serve the fish with boiled florets.

Time:47 minutes | Serves 4

Net carbs: 5% (4g/0.14oz) | Fiber: 1% (1g/0.03oz) | Fat: 64% (59g/2oz)

Protein: 30% (27g/0.95oz) | Kcal: 661

INGREDIENTS:

- ♦ 8 oz spinach
- ♦ 5 oz diced bacon
- ♦ 5 oz shredded cheese
- ♦ 2 tbsp butter
- ♦ 8 eggs
- ♦ 1 cup heavy whipping cream
- ♦ Salt and pepper

PREPARATION:

1. Preheat the oven to 175-degrees Centigrade.

2. Fry the bacon with butter until it turns crispy. Add the spinach.

3. Whisk the eggs with cream and then pour this mixture into a greased baking dish.

4. Top it with spinach, bacon and cheese. Bake for 30 minutes and then serve.

SNACKS & DESSERTS

Time: 45 minutes | Serves 4

Net carbs: 7% (7g/0.3oz) | Fiber: 4% (4g/0.14oz) | Fat: 62% (68g/2.4oz)

Protein: 27% (29g/1oz) | Kcal: 764

INGREDIENTS:

- ♦ 1 lb sausage
- ♦ 2 eggs
- ♦ 3 oz butter
- ♦ 1½ cups shredded cheese
- ♦ ½ cup almond flour
- ♦ 1 tsp baking powder
- ♦ 4 tbsp coconut flour
- ♦ ½ tsp salt

PREPARATION:

1. Preheat the oven to 175-degrees Centigrade.

2. Combine coconut flour, almond flour and baking powder.

3. Melt cheese and butter at low heat with thorough stirring.

4. To prepare the dough, whisk the egg and add flour mixture to it.

5. Shape it into a rectangle and cut out 8 strips.

6. Wrap each hot dog with the dough strip and brush with egg.

7. Bake for 20 minutes.

Time: 15 minutes | Serves 4

Net carbs: 3% (2g/0.07oz) | Fiber: 0% (0g/0oz) | Fat: 70% (19g/0.7oz)

Protein: 27% (13g/0.46oz) | Kcal: 228

INGREDIENTS:

- 8 oz shredded cheddar/ edam/provolone cheese
- ½ tsp paprika powder

PREPARATION:

1. Preheat the oven to 200-degrees Centigrade.

2. Place heaps of cheese on a lined baking sheet. Top each with some paprika powder and bake for 10 minutes.

3. Cool them down and serve the crunchy snack with a dip.

Time:18 minutes | Serves 6

Net carbs: 5% (2g/0.07oz) | Fiber: 10% (4g/0.14oz) | Fat: 74% (29g/1oz)

Protein: 10% (4g/0.14oz) | Kcal: 281

INGREDIENTS:

- ◆ 8 oz almonds
- ◆ 1 tbsp coconut oil
- ◆ 1 tsp ground cumin
- ◆ 1 tsp paprika powder
- ◆ 1tsp salt

PREPARATION:

1. Mix all the ingredients and cook it at medium heat.

2. When it cools down, serve with a drink. You can even store it for later use.

Time:12 minutes | Serves 6

Net carbs: 5% (2g/0.07oz) | Fiber: 8% (3g/0.1oz) | Fat: 75% (28g/1oz)

Protein: 11% (4g/0.14oz) | Kcal: 271

INGREDIENTS:

- ♦ 5 oz hazelnuts
- ♦ 1 oz unsalted butter
- ♦ ¼ cup coconut oil
- ♦ 2 tbsp cocoa powder
- ♦ 1 tsp vanilla extract

PREPARATION:

1. Roast the nuts and then place them on a clean towel.

2. Rub them to remove the shells.

3. Blend the resulting nuts with the remaining ingredients as long as you it doesn't attain the desired consistency.

Time:2 hours | Serves 6

Net carbs: 3% (2g/0.07oz) | Fiber: 0% (0g/0oz) | Fat: 93% (29g/1oz)

Protein: 4% (3g/0.1oz) | Kcal: 270

INGREDIENTS:

- 12 raspberries
- 2 cups heavy whipping cream
- ½ cup water
- 1 tbsp chopped almonds
- 1 tbsp honey
- ½ tbsp unflavored powdered gelatin
- ¼ tsp vanilla extract
- Pinch of saffron

PREPARATION:

1. Combine gelatin with water.

2. Heat up cream, saffron, vanilla and honey in a saucepan to reach boiling point.

3. After letting it simmer for a few minutes, add gelatin and stir.

4. Transfer it into 6 glasses and cover with plastic. Let it sit in the refrigerator for at leat 2 hours.

5. Serve each with toasted almonds, panna cotta and berries on top.

Introduction:

To get you started on the exciting and delicious journey of ketogenic diet, we have prepared a 45-day long meal plan for you. We will make sure you never go to bed hungry or stay exhausted for the day. Invest in these diverse range of mouth-watering and healthy meals to get through each day.

DAY 1

Breakfast: *Coconut Pancakes*

Serves 4 | 28 min

Net carbs: 6% (3g/0.1oz) | Fiber: 17% (8g/0.3oz) | Fat: 51% (24g/0.85oz)
Protein: 26% (12g/0.4oz) | kcal: 290

INGREDIENTS:

- 6 eggs
- ¾ cup coconut milk
- ½ cup coconut flour
- 2 tbsp melted coconut oil
- 1 tsp baking powder
- Pinch of salt
- Butter
- Berries for serving

PREPARATION:

1. Whip egg whites and mix in the salt.

2. Whisk yolks, coconut milk and oil in another bowl. Add baking powder and coconut flour to prepare a smooth batter.

3. Fold the salted egg whites into batter and leave it for 5 minutes.

4. Fry with butter on each side.

5. Serve with fresh berries.

Lunch: *Sauteed Squash with Onions & Tomatoes*

Dinner: *Chicken Casserole*

DAY 2

Breakfast: *Cloud Bread BLT*

Lunch: *Caesar Salad*

Serves 2 | 35 min
Net carbs: 3% (4g/0.14oz) | Fiber: 2% (3g/0.1oz) | Fat: 60% (86g/3oz)
Protein: 35% (47g/1.7oz) | kcal: 993

INGREDIENTS

- 10 oz chicken breasts
- 7 oz Romaine lettuce
- 3 oz bacon
- 1 finely chopped garlic clove
- 1 oz grated parmesan cheese
- 2 tbsp finely chopped anchovies fillets
- ½ cup mayonnaise
- 1 tbsp olive oil
- 1 tbsp dijon mustard
- Zest and juice of half a lemon
- Salt and pepper

PREPARATION:

1. Mix mayonnaise, mustard, lemon juice, anchovies, garlic cloves, salt, pepper and 2 tbsp parmesan cheese to create the dressing.

2. Preheat the oven to 200-degrees Centigrade and grease the baking dish.

3. Season the chicken breasts with salt, pepper and olive oil. Bake them on the greased dish for 20 minutes.

4. Spread the lettuce on plate and arrange the cooked chicken.

5. Make the bacon crispy by frying. Then use it as topping on the chicken, along with dressing and 1 oz parmesan cheese.

Dinner: *Garlic Asiago Cauliflower Rice*

DAY 3

Breakfast: *Bulletproof Coffee*

Lunch: *Mixed Spice Burgers*

Dinner: *Keto Salmon Pie*

Serves 4 | 50min
Net carbs: 3% (6g/0.2oz) | Fiber: 4% (7g/0.3oz) | Fat: 58% (101g/3.5oz)
Protein: 34% (58g/2oz) | kcal: 1179

INGREDIENTS

- 8 oz smoked salmon
- 4¼ oz cream cheese
- 4 eggs
- 1¼ cups shredded cheese
- 1 cup mayonnaise
- ¾ cup almond flour
- 4 tbsp coconut flour
- 4 tbsp sesame seeds
- 4 tbsp water
- 2 tbsp finely chopped dill
- 3 tbsp olive oil
- 1 tsp baking powder
- 1 tbsp ground psyllium husk powder
- ½ tsp onion powder
- Pinch of salt and pepper

PREPARATION:

1. Preheat the oven to 175-degrees Centigrade.
2. Mix almond flour, coconut flour, psyllium husk powder, baking powder, sesame seeds, water, olive oil, an egg and some salt to prepare the pie dough.
3. Press this dough gently with oil on a spring form pan. Pre-bake it for 12 minutes.
4. Mix rest of the ingredients except salmon to prepare the pie filling. Then pour it inside the pie crust.
5. Add salmon on top and bake for until the pie turns golden brown.
6. Serve when cooled down with salad or veggies.

DAY 4

Breakfast: *Cauliflower Hash Browns*

Serves 4 | 30 min

Net carbs: 12% (5g/0.18oz) | Fiber: 6% (3g/0.1oz) | Fat: 63% (26g/0.9oz)
Protein: 17% (7g/0.3oz) | kcal: 278

INGREDIENTS

- 15 oz grated cauliflower
- 4 oz butter
- 3 eggs
- 1 tsp salt
- ½ grated yellow onion
- Pinches of pepper

PREPARATION:

1. Combine all the ingredients in a bowl and leave for 10 minutes.

2. Melt butter in a skillet at medium heat. Place the cauliflower mixture in scoops on it and gently flatten them.

3. Fry for a few minutes.

Lunch: *Cabbage Roll Soup*

Dinner: *Turkey with Cream-Cheese Sauce*

Breakfast: *Pancakes with Cream and Berries*

Lunch: *Chicken Tonnato*

Serves **4** | 35 min

Net carbs: 2% (2g/0.07oz) | Fiber: 2% (2g/0.07oz) | Fat: 52% (54g/1.9oz)

Protein: 44% (46g/1.6oz) | kcal: 687

INGREDIENTS

- 25 oz chicken breasts
- 7 oz leafy greens
- 4 oz tuna in olive oil
- ½ cup mayonnaise
- ¼ cup chopped basil
- ¼ cup olive oil
- 2 garlic cloves
- 2 tbsp lemon juice
- 1 tsp parsley
- ½ tsp salt
- ¼ tsp ground black pepper
- Water

PREPARATION:

1. Combine everything except chicken, water and leafy greens to prepare the tonnato sauce. The longer you store it, the tastier it will get.

2. Fill up a pot with slightly salted water so that it covers the chicken breasts. When the temperature reaches boiling point, remove the foam from its surface. Let the chicken simmer for 15 minutes.

3. Transfer the cooked chicken breasts to another place and let them sit for 10 minutes.

4. Slice up the chicken and serve them on top of leafy greens. Spread the tonnato sauce over each piece before eating.

Dinner: *Cajun Sirloin with Mushroom Leek Sauce*

DAY 6

Breakfast: *Eggs and Bacon*

Lunch: *Brussel Sprouts with Goat Cheese*

Dinner: *Chicken Korma*

Serves 3 | 45 min

Net carbs: 7% (6g/0.2oz) | Fiber: 2% (2g/0.07oz) | Fat: 65% (48g/1.7oz)

Protein: 33% (27g/0.95oz) | kcal: 568

INGREDIENTS

- 15 oz chicken drumsticks and thighs
- 4 oz Greek yogurt
- 1 thinly sliced red onion
- 3 whole cloves
- 8 whole black peppercorns
- 3 green cardamom pods
- 1 cinnamon stick
- 1 bay leaf
- 4 tbsp ghee
- 1 star anise
- 1 tsp ground cumin
- 1 tsp ground coriander seed
- 1 tsp ginger garlic paste
- 1 tsp kashmiri red chilli powder
- ½ tsp turmeric
- ½ garam masala
- Salt & cilantro

PREPARATION:

1. Fry the onions in ghee so that they turn golden brown.

2. Blend these onions with yogurt to form a creamy paste.

3. Heat up the ghee again in saucepan. Now fry cinnamon stick, cardamom pods, cloves, black peppercorns, bay leaf and star anise until they sizzle.

4. Now add the drumsticks and thighs. Stir in ginger garlic paste and salt for better taste.

5. Add all the spices and cook for a while.

6. Now introduce the yogurt paste and mix them all together well. Add some water as well.

7. Cook it for 12 minutes with the lid on.

8. Serve with cilantro on top and a side dish of rice.

DAY 7

Breakfast: *Croque Monsieur*

Serves 4 | 23 min

Net carbs: 5% (8g/0.3oz) | Fiber: 2.5% (4g/0.14oz) | Fat: 58% (92g/3oz)

Protein: 34% (54g/1.8oz) | kcal: 1082

INGREDIENTS

- 15 oz cottage cheese
- 10 oz cheddar cheese
- 10 oz smoked deli ham
- 7 oz lettuce
- 8 eggs
- 1 finely chopped red onion
- 8 tbsp butter
- 8 tbsp olive oil
- 2 tbsp ground psyllium husk powder
- 1 tbsp red wine vinegar
- Salt and pepper

PREPARATION:

1. Mix whisked eggs and cottage cheese with the psyllium husk powder. Make sure the mixture is free of lumps.

2. Fry portions of the batter at medium heat.

3. Take two of these cooked pancakes. Fill up the space between them with sliced ham and cheese. Top each with some finely chopped onions.

4. Prepare a vinaigrette with vinegar, salt, pepper and oil.

5. Serve with vinaigrette and lettuce.

Lunch: *Parmesan Chicken*

Dinner: *Shrimp Scampi Spinach Salad*

DAY 8

Breakfast: *Mushroom Omelet*

Lunch: *Spicy Shrimp Salad*

Serves 2 | 11 min

Net carbs: 7% (9g/0.3oz) | Fiber: 12% (16g/0.6oz) | Fat: 60% (79g/2.8oz)

Protein: 20% (26g/0.9oz) | kcal: 870

INGREDIENTS

- 10 oz peeled shrimp
- 5 oz peeled and sliced cucumber
- 2 oz baby spinach
- 2 halved and sliced avocados
- 1 + ½ pressed garlic cloves
- ¼ cup light olive oil
- 1 tbsp minced ginger
- 3 tbsp olive oil
- 2 tsp chili powder
- ½ tbsp tamari soy sauce
- Juice of a lemon
- Cilantro
- Salt and pepper

PREPARATION:

1. Drizzle some lemon juice on the avocado slices. Prepare a mixture of these avocado slices, cucumber slices and spinach. Toss with sea salt.

2. Fry garlic and chilli in olive oil. Then cook the shrimp in it for 5 minutes. Add salt and pepper.

3. Add this cooked shrimp to the previous vegetable mixture. Add nuts and cilantro for topping.

4. Prepare the dressing by blending tamari soy sauce, ½ garlic clove, ginger, light olive oil, salt, pepper and rest of lime juice. Spread some of this dressing on the salad.

Dinner: *Chicken and Broccoli with Dill Sauce*

DAY 9

Breakfast: *Blueberry Smoothie*

Lunch: *Parmesan Tilapia*

Dinner: *Zucchini Crusted Pizza*

Serves 6 | 40 min
Net carbs: 25% (9g/0.3oz) | Fiber: 3% (1g/0.03oz) | Fat: 33% (12g/0.4oz)
Protein: 39% (14g/0.5oz) | kcal: 219

INGREDIENTS

- 3 lightly beaten eggs
- 12 oz julienned roasted sweet peppers
- 2 cups shredded zucchini
- ½ cup grated Parmesan cheese
- 1 cup shredded part-skim mozzarella cheese
- ½ cup sliced turkey pepperoni
- ¼ cup all purpose flour
- 1 tbsp minced thyme
- 1 tbsp olive oil
- 1 tbsp minced basil

PREPARATION:

1. Preheat oven to 450-degrees.

2. Mix all ingredients except peppers and pepperoni.

3. Now spread the mixture on a coated pizza pan. Bake for 15 minutes.

4. Lower the oven temperature to 400-degrees. Top it with pepperoni, peppers and more cheese if you like. Now bake again for 10 more minutes.

DAY 10

Breakfast: *French Toast*

Serves 2 | 10 min

Net carbs: 6% (4g/0.14oz) | Fiber: 6% (4g/0.14oz) | Fat: 62% (37g/1.3oz)

Protein: 25% (15g/0.5oz) | kcal: 416

INGREDIENTS

- 4 tbsp heavy whipping cream
- 4 eggs
- 3 tbsp butter
- 2 tbsp coconut flour
- 2 tbsp almond flour
- 1½ tsp baking powder
- ½ tsp ground cinnamon
- Pinches of salt

PREPARATION:

1. Grease the bottom of a glass dish with 1 tsp butter.

2. Mix the flours, baking powder and some salt in a mug. Then add in 2 eggs and half the cream to make a smooth texture.

3. Microwave it for 2 minutes. When the bread is done, slice them in half.

4. Mix the rest of eggs, cinnamon, cream and salt in a bowl. Rub this mixture on the bread slices.

5. Fry the slices in butter and serve fresh.

Lunch: *Creamed Green Cabbage and Chorizo*

Dinner: *Simple Keto Pizza*

DAY 11

Breakfast: *Coconut Porridge*

Lunch: *Quesadillas*

Serves 3 | 30 min
Net carbs: 7% (5g/0.2oz)
Fiber: 4% (3g/0.1oz)
Fat: 58% (41g/1.44oz)
Protein: 30% (21g/0.74oz)
kcal: 474

INGREDIENTS

- 6 oz cream cheese
- 5 oz Mexican cheese
- 1 oz baby spinach
- 2 egg whites
- 2 eggs
- 1 tbsp coconut flour
- 1 tbsp butter
- 1½ tsp ground psyllium husk powder
- ½ tsp salt

PREPARATION:

1. Preheat the oven to 200-degrees Centigrade.

2. Beat the egg whites and eggs so that they get a fluffy texture. Then add cream cheese to it and keep beating.

3. Mix coconut flour, salt and psyllium husk in another bowl.

4. Add this mixture to the batter. Leave it for a while so that the consistency becomes thicker.

5. Shape the batter on parchment paper in the form of a rectangle.

6. Bake it for 10 minutes on the upper rack. Then cut it into 6 pieces of tortilla.

7. Melt butter on a non-stick skillet. Place each tortilla on it. Top the tortilla with cheese and spinach. Fry until the cheese melts.

Dinner: *Keto crab meat and egg plate*

DAY 12

Breakfast: *Smoked Salmon Sandwich*

Lunch: *Lettuce Sandwich*

Dinner: *Rutabaga Fritters with Bacon*

Serves 4 | 20 min
Net carbs: 8% (11g/0.4oz)
Fiber: 5% (7g/0.3oz)
Fat: 68% (92g/3.5oz)
Protein: 18% (24g/0.85oz)
kcal: 978

INGREDIENTS

- 4 eggs
- 15 oz peeled and grated rutabaga
- 6 oz bacon
- 6 oz grated halloumi cheese
- 5⅓ oz leafy greens
- 3 oz butter
- 1 cup mayonnaise
- 3 tbsp coconut flour
- 1 tsp salt
- ½ tsp onion powder
- ¼ tsp pepper
- ⅛ tsp turmeric

PREPARATION:

1. Combine all ingredients except bacon, leafy greens and mayonnaise. Make 12 patties out of it and arrange in a frying pan heated with butter.

2. Fry the patties. Serve each patty with mayonnaise, leafy greens and bacon.

DAY 13

Breakfast: *Scrambled Eggs with Basil and Butter*

Serves 1 | 5 min

Net carbs: 3% (2g/0.07oz) | Fiber: 2% (1g/0.03oz) | Fat: 72% (42g/1.5oz)
Protein: 22% (13g/0.46oz) | kcal: 427

INGREDIENTS

- 2 eggs
- 1 oz butter
- 2 tbsp coconut cream
- 2 tbsp basil
- Salt and shredded cheese

PREPARATION:

1. Whisk eggs, cream and salt in a bowl.

2. Melt butter in a pan. Then add the egg mixture to it.

3. Keep stirring at low heat to reach a soft and creamy texture for the scrambled eggs.

Lunch: *Red Pepper, Asparagus & Squash Saute*

Dinner: *Thai Fish Curry with Coconut*

Breakfast: *Huevos Rancheros*

Lunch: *Fried Chicken with Broccoli*

Serves 2 | 20 min
Net carbs: 5% (5g/0.2oz) | Fiber: 3% (3g/0.1oz) | Fat: 60% (66g/2.3oz)
Protein: 27% (29g/1oz) | kcal: 733

INGREDIENTS

- 10 oz boneless chicken thighs
- 9 oz trimmed and diced broccoli
- 3½ oz butter
- ⅓ cup mayonnaise
- Salt and pepper

PREPARATION:

1. Drop one portion of butter in the pan.

2. Season chicken with salt and pepper. Fry each of the pieces until they turn golden brown on both sides.

3. Add more butter and broccoli. Fry for couple more minutes.

4. Season with salt and pepper. Serve with the remaining butter.

Dinner: *Frittata with Spinach*

DAY 15

Breakfast: *Scrambled Eggs*

Lunch: *Cabbage Roll Soup*

Dinner: *White Pizza with Mushrooms and Pesto*

Serves 4 | 32 min

Net carbs: 5% (7g/0.3oz) | Fiber: 2% (4g/0.14oz) | Fat: 74% (110g/4oz)
Protein: 18% (27g/0.95oz) | kcal: 1147

INGREDIENTS

- 4 eggs
- 4 oz thinly sliced mushrooms
- 1½ cups almond flour
- 1½ cups shredded cheese
- 1 cup sour cream
- 2 tbsp green pesto
- 1 cup mayonnaise
- 2 tbsp ground psyllium husk powder
- 4 tbsp olive oil
- 2 tsp baking powder
- 1⅛ tsp salt
- Pepper

PREPARATION:

1. Preheat the oven to 175-degrees Centigrade.

2. Whisk eggs with mayonnaise. Then add almond flour, psyllium husk powder, baking powder and 1 tsp salt to form the batter.

3. Spread the batter on a baking sheet. Then bake it until the crust turns light golden brown.

4. Layer the cooked crust with sour cream.

5. Combine mushrooms, pesto , salt, pepper and olive oil. Spread this mixture on the sour cream layer.

6. Bake this again for 10 minutes.

DAY 16

Breakfast: *Biscuits and Gravy*

Serves 8 | 25 min
Net carbs: 6% (3g/0.1oz) | Fiber: 0% (0g/0oz) | Fat: 67% (33g/1.16oz)
Protein: 26% (13g/0.46oz) | kcal: 358

INGREDIENTS

- 10 oz crumbled sausage
- 4 egg whites
- 1 cup almond flour
- 1 cup broth (beef/chicken)
- 1 cup coconut cream
- 2 tbsp cold butter
- 1 tsp baking powder
- 1 tsp coconut oil spray
- 1 tsp garlic powder
- ¼ tsp sea salt
- Pepper

PREPARATION:

1. Preheat the oven to 200-degrees Centigrade.
2. Combine almond flour and baking powder in a bowl.
3. Keep beating the eggs in another bowl to reach a fluffy texture.
4. Cut in salt and cold butter.
5. Fold the mixture into egg whites.
6. Place scoops of dough on a greased cookie sheet and bake for 15 minutes.

Lunch: *Sauteed Squash with Onions & Tomatoes*

Dinner: *Chicken Casserole*

DAY 17

Breakfast: *Pancakes with Cream and Berries*

Lunch: *Cauliflower Hash with Eggs*

Serves 2 | 25 min

Net carbs: 7% (9g/0.3oz) | Fiber: 5% (6g/0.2oz) | Fat: 72% (87g/3oz)
Protein: 14% (17g/0.6oz) | kcal: 898

INGREDIENTS

- 4 eggs
- 1 lb grated cauliflower
- 3 oz poblano peppers (pimientos de padron)
- 3 oz butter
- ½ cup mayonnaise
- 1 tsp olive oil
- 1 tsp garlic powder
- Salt and pepper

PREPARATION:

1. Fry the cauliflower in butter for a few minutes and season it with salt-pepper.

2. Rub the peppers with some oil and grill them.

3. Fry the eggs with salt and pepper.

4. Mix garlic powder and mayonnaise to serve as dip alongside the cauliflower has and roasted poblanos.

Dinner: *Turkey with Cream-Cheese Sauce*

DAY 18

Breakfast: *Eggs and Bacon*

Lunch: *Carrot, Radish and Cilantro Salad*

Dinner: *Thai Fish with Curry and Coconut*

Serves 4 | 30 min
Net carbs: 7% (9g/0.3oz) | Fiber: 3% (5g/0.18oz) | Fat: 57% (75g/2.6oz)
Protein: 32% (42g/1.5oz) | kcal: 880

INGREDIENTS

- 25 oz white fish, cut into pieces
- 15 oz broccoli
- 14 oz coconut cream
- 1 oz olive oil
- ½ cup chopped cilantro
- 4 tbsp butter
- 2 tbsp green curry paste
- Salt and pepper

PREPARATION:

1. Preheat the oven to 200-degrees Centigrade. Grease the baking dish with olive oil.

2. Put the fish pieces on the dish. Top each piece with some salt, pepper and 1 tbsp butter.

3. Combine curry paste, coconut cream and cilantro. Add this mixture on the pieces.

4. Bake for 20 minutes. Boil broccoli in salted water and serve alongside.

DAY 19

Breakfast: *Soft Tortillas*

Serves 12 | 40 min
Net carbs: 4% (2g/0.07oz) | Fiber: 34% (15g/0.5oz) | Fat: 48% (21g/0.74oz)
Protein: 14% (6g/0.2oz) | kcal: 250

INGREDIENTS

- ♦ 6 large egg whites
- ♦ 3 cups hot water
- ♦ 2 cups coconut flour
- ♦ 1 cup olive oil
- ♦ ½ cup ground psyllium husk powder
- ♦ 1 tsp salt
- ♦ ½ tsp baking soda

PREPARATION:

1. Mix baking soda, coconut flour, salt and psyllium husk powder in a bowl.

2. Add the oil slowly afterwards to make it a little moist.

3. Add egg whites and hot water too but very carefully. The water should be added in no more than half a cup at once.

4. Shape into 12 or 24 balls depending on how thin or thick you want them to be. Press them enough to get the required thickness.

5. Cook them in batches and toast each side for 3 minutes.

Lunch: *Brussel Sprouts with Goat Cheese*

Dinner: *Cajun Sirloin with Mushroom Leek Sauce*

DAY 20

Breakfast: *Bulletproof Coffee*

Lunch: *Fried Cheese with Roasted Pepper*

Serves 4 | 35 min
Net carbs: 7% (10g/0.35oz) | Fiber: 2% (3g/0.1oz) | Fat: 69% (99g/3.5oz)
Protein: 22% (31g/1.1oz) | kcal: 1061

INGREDIENTS

- 15 oz red bell peppers
- 20 oz halloumi cheese
- 3 oz cream cheese
- 2 oz chopped dill pickles
- 2 oz diced cucumber
- ¾ cup mayonnaise
- 2 tsp dried mint
- ½ cup olive oil
- ½ tsp salt
- 1 tsp dried oregano
- ¼ tsp ground black pepper

PREPARATION:

1. Preheat the oven to 225-degrees Centigrade. The broil function will suit this dish better.

2. Broil the bell peppers on a baking sheet for 12 minutes.

3. Mix everything else except olive oil, oregano and halloumi cheese to prepare the cucumber salad. Refrigerate it for later use.

4. Fry halloumi cheese with olive oil. Then serve this fried cheese, bell peppers and the cucumber salad on the same plate.

Dinner: *Shrimp Scampi Spinach Salad*

DAY 21

Breakfast: *Coconut Porridge*

Lunch: *Creamed Green Cabbage and Chorizo*

Dinner: *Garlic Chicken*

Serves 4 |50 min
Net carbs: 3% (4g/0.14oz) | Fiber: 1% (1g/0.03oz) | Fat: 30% (39g/1.4oz)
Protein: 35% (42g/1.5oz) | kcal: 546

INGREDIENTS

- 2 lbs chicken drumsticks
- 5 sliced garlic cloves
- ½ cup finely chopped parsley
- 2 tbsp olive oil
- 4 tbsp butter
- Juice of a lemon

PREPARATION:

1. Preheat the oven to 225-degrees Centigrade. Grease the baking pan with butter.

2. Arrange the drumsticks on this pan. Top them with salt, pepper, garlic, parsley, olive oil and lemon juice.

3. Bake for a little bit over half an hour.

DAY 22

Breakfast: *Baked Eggs Ratatouille*

Serves 4 | 25 min

Net carbs: 15% (11g/0.4oz) | Fiber: 10% (7g/0.3oz) | Fat: 53% (38g/1.34oz)

Protein: 21% (15g/0.5oz) | kcal: 460

INGREDIENTS

- 8 eggs
- 1 thinly sliced green chili pepper
- 1 sliced eggplant
- 1 sliced green bell pepper
- 1 sliced zucchini
- 1 sliced yellow onion
- 1 minced garlic clove
- 400g strained tomatoes
- ½ cup olives
- 4 tbsp olive oil
- 2 tsp paprika powder
- 2 tsp cilantro

PREPARATION:

1. Saute all the vegetables in olive oil. Add spices, salt, pepper and garlic to season it.

2. Add tomatoes later and simmer the whole concoction for approximately half an hour.

3. Carve holes into the dish and crack an egg into each hole.

4. Let it simmer being covered for 10 minutes. To cook the eggs even better, you can bake it further in oven for a while.

5. Serve with sliced chili, olives and some more olive oil.

Lunch: *Parmesan Chicken*

Dinner: *Simple Keto Pizza*

DAY 23

Breakfast: *Huevos Rancheros*

Lunch: *Cabbage Soup with chicken Dumplings*

Serves 4 | 35 min
Net carbs: 4% (6g/0.2oz) | Fiber: 2% (3g/0.1oz) | Fat: 40% (46g/1.7oz)
Protein: 20% (25g/0.9oz) | kcal: 541

INGREDIENTS

- 1 lb cored and chopped green cabbage
- 1 lb ground chicken
- 6 oz butter
- 1 large egg
- 6 cups chicken broth
- 4 tbsp chopped parsley
- 1 tsp onion powder
- 1¼ tsp salt
- ⅔ tsp ground black pepper
- ¼ tsp ground nutmeg

PREPARATION:

1. Prepare the parsley butter with 4 oz butter, 1 tbsp parsley, pinch of salt and pepper.

2. Combine the ground chicken, cabbage, rest of parsley, onion powder, ground nutmeg and ½ tsp salt to prepare the dumpling mixture. Refrigerate this for 10 minutes.

3. Shape this mixture into several balls.

4. Let the butter melt at low heat in a big pot. Cook the cabbage here at a slightly higher temperature so that it turns tender.

5. Add chicken broth, let it reach boiling temperature and then lower the heat.

6. Introduce the dumpling balls and simmer for 10 minutes. Add salt and pepper for seasoning.

7. Serve the dumpling soup with parsley butter.

Dinner: *Thai Fish Curry with Coconut*

DAY 24

Breakfast: *Smoked Salmon Sandwich*

Lunch: *Parmesan Chicken*

Dinner: *Shakshuka*

Serves 4 | 30 min
Net carbs: 16% (4g/0.14oz) | Fiber: 8% (2g/0.07oz) | Fat: 48% (12g/0.4oz)
Protein: 28% (7g/0.3oz) | kcal: 159

INGREDIENTS

- 1 tsp pepper
- 2 chopped tomatoes
- 4 large eggs
- 1 minced garlic clove
- 2 tbsp olive oil
- 1 chopped onion
- 1 tsp ground cumin
- 1 tsp hot pepper sauce
- ½ tsp salt
- ½ tsp chili powder
- Toasted whole pita breads
- Chopped cilantro

PREPARATION:

1. Fry onion in olive oil for 5 minutes. Add in garlic, chili sauce and seasonings. Stir for a few seconds before adding tomatoes. Cook for 5 more minutes.

2. Press on four areas of this concoction to make space for eggs. Then crack one egg per well. Cook for 5 minutes so that the eggs can set.

3. Throw some cilantro on top and serve with bread.

DAY 25

Breakfast: *English Muffins*

Serves 3 | 15 min

Net carbs: 4% (1g/0.03oz) | Fiber: 12% (3g/0.1oz) | Fat: 62% (15g/0.5oz)
Protein: 21% (5g/0.18oz) | kcal: 159

INGREDIENTS

- 2 eggs
- 3 tbsp coconut oil
- ½ tsp baking powder
- 2 tbsp coconut flour
- Pinch of salt

PREPARATION:

1. Combine baking powder, coconut flour and salt. Add eggs to it and whisk the whole mixture.

2. Melt butter on the frying pan. Spoon three portions of the batter on it and cook at medium high.

3. Prepare all the muffins like this and serve with butter.

Lunch: *Red Pepper, Asparagus & Squash Saute*

Dinner: *Chicken Casserole*

DAY 26

Breakfast: *Cloud Bread BLT*

Lunch: *Grilled Veggie Plate*

Serves 4 | 30 min

Net carbs: 6% (9g/0.3oz) | Fiber: 4% (6g/0.2oz) | Fat: 73% (99g/3.5oz)

Protein: 16% (21g/0.74oz) | kcal: 1013

INGREDIENTS

- 20 black olives
- 1 sliced zucchini
- ⅔ sliced eggplant
- 10 oz cheddar cheese
- 2 oz leafy greens
- 1 cup mayonnaise
- ½ cup olive oil
- 4 tbsp almonds
- Juice of a lemon
- Salt and pepper

PREPARATION:

1. Salt the eggplant and zucchini slices on both sides. Leave them like this for 5 minutes.

2. Set the oven to broil. Place those slices on a baking sheet. Brush them with olive oil and add pepper for seasoning.

3. Broil them until they turn golden brown.

4. Serve fresh with some olive oil, lemon juice, cheese cubes, mayonnaise, leafy greens, almonds and olives.

Dinner: *Turkey with Cream-Cheese Sauce*

DAY 27

Breakfast: *Pancakes with Cream and Berries*

Lunch: *Carrot, Radish and Cilantro Salad*

Dinner: *Flying Jacob Casserole*

Serves 6 | 40 min

Net carbs: 8% (11g/0.4oz) | Fiber: 2% (3g/0.1oz) | Fat: 58% (80g/2.8oz)

Protein: 30% (40g/1.4oz) | kcal: 912

INGREDIENTS

- 1 deboned rotisserie chicken, cut into pieces
- 2 diced tomatoes
- 1 sliced banana
- 9 oz mushrooms, cut into pieces
- 8 oz diced bacon
- 6 oz baby spinach
- 2 cups heavy whipping cream
- ½ cup salted peanuts
- ½ cup mild chili sauce
- 2 tbsp butter
- 1 tsp curry powder
- Salt and pepper

PREPARATION:

1. Preheat the oven to 200-degrees Centigrade.

2. Fry the mushrooms and bacon in butter, salt and pepper.

3. Put the chicken pieces on a greased baking dish. Add the cooked mushrooms and sliced banana to it.

4. Keep whisking the whipping cream until you see peaks forming. Then add salt, curry and chili sauce to it. Spread this combination over the chicken.

5. Bake for half an hour. Serve with fresh salad and toppings of chopped peanuts.

DAY 28

Breakfast: *Keto Bread*

Serves 6 | 1 hour 10 min
Net carbs: 7% (2g/0.07oz) | Fiber: 21% (6g/0.2oz) | Fat: 46% (13g/0.46oz)
Protein: 25% (7g/0.3oz) | kcal: 170

INGREDIENTS

- 3 egg whites
- 1¼ cups almond flour
- 1 cup boiling water
- 5 tbsp ground psyllium husk powder
- 2 tbsp sesame seeds
- 2 tsp cider vinegar
- 2 tsp baking powder
- 1 tsp sea salt

PREPARATION:

1. Preheat the oven to 175-degrees Centigrade.

2. Combine the dry ingredients. Then add egg whites and vinegar to the mixture.

3. Add the boiling water such that it reaches the perfect consistency for a dough.

4. Damp your hands with some olive oil and shape dough into rolls.

5. Grease a baking dish and place the rolls on it. Top each with sesame seeds.

6. Bake the rolls for an hour.

7. Serve with butter.

Lunch: *Mixed Spice Burgers*

Dinner: *Frittata with Spinach*

DAY 29

Breakfast: *Mushroom Omelet*

Lunch: *Goat Cheese Salad with Balsamic Butter*

Serves 2/15 min
Net carbs: 3% (3g/0.1oz) | Fiber: 2% (2g/0.07oz) | Fat: 63% (73g/2.6oz)
Protein: 32% (37g/1.3oz) | kcal: 824

INGREDIENTS

- 10 oz sliced goat cheese
- 3 oz baby spinach
- 2 oz butter
- ¼ cup pumpkin seeds
- 1 tbsp balsamic vinegar

PREPARATION:

1. Preheat the oven to 200-degrees Centigrade.

2. Bake the cheese slices on a greased baking dish for 10 minutes.

3. Toast the pumpkin seeds without any moisture until they start popping at high temperature.

4. Then decrease the temperature, add butter and simmer it until a golden brown color appears.

5. Add vinegar to the mixture and let it boil for 5 more minutes.

6. Serve the spinach with cheese and balsamic butter.

Dinner: *Turkey with Cream-Cheese Sauce*

DAY 30

Breakfast: *Blueberry Smoothie*

Lunch: *Cabbage Roll Soup*

Dinner: *Baked Salmon with Butter and Lemon*

Serves 6 | 35 min
Net carbs: 1% (1g/0.03oz) | Fiber: 0% (0g/0z) | Fat: 60% (49g/1.7oz)
Protein: 39% (31g/1.1oz) | kcal: 573

INGREDIENTS

- 2 lbs salmon
- 7 oz butter
- 1 sliced lemon
- 1 tbsp olive oil
- 1 tsp sea salt
- Ground black pepper
- Lemon juice

PREPARATION:

1. Preheat the oven to 200-degrees Centigrade.

2. Place salmon on a olive-oil greased baking dish. Add salt and pepper for seasoning. Top with half the butter and lemon slices.

3. Bake for half an hour on middle rack.

4. Take the remaining butter in another pan and heat it up until bubbles form. Then take it away from stove and add lemon juice.

5. Serve the salmon with this lemon butter.

DAY 31

Breakfast: *Parmesan Croutons*

Serves 8 | 1 hour

Net carbs: 3% (1g/0.03oz) | Fiber: 12% (4g/0.14oz) | Fat: 62% (21g/0.74oz)
Protein: 24% (8g/0.3oz) | kcal: 238

INGREDIENTS

- 3 oz butter
- 3 egg whites
- 2 oz grated parmesan cheese
- 1¼ cups almond flour
- 1¼ cups boiling water
- 5 tbsp ground psyllium husk powder
- 2 tsp cider vinegar
- 2 tsp baking powder
- 1 tsp sea salt

PREPARATION:

1. Preheat the oven to 175-degrees Centigrade.

2. First combine all the dry ingredients. Then add the boiling water, egg white and vinegar to it. Beat up for half a minute to reach the perfect dough-like consistency.

3. Shape up 8 flat pieces from the dough. Bake them for 40 minutes on the lower oven rack.

4. Cut each bread piece into half.

5. Mix parmesan cheese and butter. Spread this one each half of bread pieces.

6. Bake them again at 220-degrees Centigrade for 5 minutes.

Lunch: *Brussel Sprouts with Goat Cheese*

Dinner: *Cajun Sirloin with Mushroom Leek Sauce*

DAY 32

Breakfast: *Coconut Porridge*

Lunch: *Spinach Artichoke Stuffed Chicken Breast*

Serves 6 | 30 min

Net carbs: 1% (2g/0.07oz) | Fiber: 1% (1g/0.03oz) | Fat: 26% (17g/0.6oz)

Protein: 56% (28g/1oz) | kcal: 288

INGREDIENTS

- 1½ lbs pounded chicken breasts
- ½ cup thinly sliced artichoke hearts
- 4 oz softened cream cheese
- ½ cup shredded mozzarella
- ¼ cup spinach
- ¼ cup Greek yogurt
- ½ tsp salt
- 2 tbsp olive oil
- ¼ tsp pepper

PREPARATION:

1. Cut the chicken breasts to make room for the filling. Then season it with half the salt and half the pepper.

2. Mix mozzarella cheese, cream cheese, yogurt, spinach and artichoke with rest of salt and pepper in another bowl.

3. Use this mixture to fill up the chicken breasts.

4. Cook them at medium heat for a total of 20 minutes.

5. You can serve it with a side of rice.

Dinner: *Shrimp Scampi Spinach Salad*

DAY 33

Breakfast: *Smoked Salmon Sandwich*

Lunch: *Parmesan Chicken*

Dinner: *Avocado Pie*

Serves 4 | 1 hour

Net carbs: 5% (9g/0.3oz) | Fiber: 9% (14g/0.5oz) | Fat: 68% (109g/3.8oz)
Protein: 16% (26g/0.9oz) | kcal: 1146

INGREDIENTS

- 4 eggs
- 2 finely chopped avocados
- 1 finely chopped red chilli pepper
- 1 cup mayonnaise
- 1¼ cups shredded cheese
- ½ cup cream cheese
- ¾ cup almond flour
- 4 tbsp coconut flour
- 4 tbsp sesame seeds
- 4 tbsp water
- 3 tbsp olive oil
- 2 tbsp finely chopped cilantro
- 1 tbsp ground psyllium husk powder
- 1 tsp baking powder
- ⅔ tsp salt
- ½ tsp onion powder

PREPARATION:

1. Preheat the oven to 175-degrees Centigrade.

2. Mix almond flour, coconut flour, baking powder, psyllium husk powder, sesame seeds, olive oil, an egg, water and some salt. This will prepare the dough for the pie crust.

3. Grease a spring form pan with parchment paper. Spread the dough on it and bake for 15 minutes.

4. Mix avocado with rest of the ingredients. Add this into the pie crust and bake for 30 minutes.

DAY 34

Breakfast: *Caprese Omelet*

Serves 2 | 20 min

Net carbs: 5% (4g/0.14oz) | Fiber: 1% (1g/0.03oz) | Fat: 53% (43g/1.5oz)

Protein: 31% (33g/1.16oz) | kcal: 534

Ingredients

- 5 oz mozzarella cheese
- 3 oz sliced tomatoes
- 6 eggs
- 1 tbsp basil
- 2 tbsp olive oil
- Salt and pepper

PREPARATION:

1. Whisk the eggs, salt, pepper and basil together.

2. Fry the tomatoes in olive oil for 5 minutes.

3. Add the egg mixture from top. When this batter turns a little more firm, introduce the cheese.

4. Reduce the temperature. When the omelet sets well, serve it fresh.

Lunch: *Creamed Green Cabbage and Chorizo*

Dinner: *Shrimp Scampi Spinach Salad*

DAY 35

Breakfast: *Huevos Rancheros*

Lunch: *Halloumi Cheese and Avocado Plate*

Serves 2 | 10 min
Net carbs: 7% (12g/0.4oz) | Fiber: 9% (14g/0.5oz) | Fat: 60% (100g/3.5oz)
Protein: 22% (36g/1.27oz) | kcal: 1112

INGREDIENTS

- 10 oz sliced halloumi cheese
- ¼ cucumber
- 2 avocados
- ¼ lemon
- ⅓ Cup sour cream
- 2 tbsp butter
- 2 tbsp olive oil
- 2 tbsp pistachio nuts
- Salt and pepper

PREPARATION:

1. Fry the cheese in butter at medium heat so that it turns golden.

2. Combine it with avocado, cucumber, pistachios, lemon and sour cream.

3. Add salt, pepper and olive oil before serving.

Dinner: *Chicken and Broccoli with Dill Sauce*

DAY 36

Breakfast: *Scrambled Eggs*

Lunch: *Lettuce Sandwich*

Dinner: *Chicken Provençale*

Serves 4 | 1 hour 10 minutes
Net carbs: 4% (5g/0.18oz) | Fiber: 2% (3g/0.1oz) | Fat: 60% (78g/2.75oz)
Protein: 33% (43g/1.5oz) | kcal: 911

INGREDIENTS

- 2 lbs chicken thighs
- 7 oz lettuce
- 8 oz tomatoes
- 5 sliced garlic cloves
- 1 cup mayonnaise
- ¼ cup olive oil
- ½ cup pitted black olives
- 1 tbsp dried oregano
- 1 tsp paprika powder
- Zest of a quarter lemon
- Salt and pepper

PREPARATION:

1. Preheat the oven to 200-degrees Centigrade.

2. Keep the chicken on an oven-proof baking dish. Place garlic, tomatoes and olives around it. Add oregano, olive oil, salt and pepper as toppings.

3. Roast it for about an hour. Make sure the internal temperature is 75-degrees Centigrade.

4. Mix mayonnaise, paprika power, lemon zest, lettuce, salt and pepper. Serve this mixture with the salad.

DAY 37

Breakfast: *Oven Pancake with Bacon*

Serves 8 | 40 min

Net carbs: 7% (5g/0.18oz) | Fiber: 3% (2g/0.07oz) | Fat:68% (50g/1.8oz)

Protein: 22% (16g/0.6oz) | kcal: 545

INGREDIENTS

- 8 eggs
- 7 oz sliced pork bacon
- 1 sliced yellow onion
- 2 cups heavy whipping cream
- 1 cup almond flour
- 1 cup cottage cheese
- 4 tbsp butter
- 2 tbsp parsley
- 2 tbsp ground psyllium husk powder
- 2 tsp salt
- 2 tsp baking powder

PREPARATION:

1. Preheat the oven to 175-degrees Centigrade.

2. Fry the onion and bacon slices in butter. Stop when the onions are tender and bacon slices are crispy.

3. Whisk eggs, cream and cottage cheese in a bowl. Then add baking powder, almond flour, salt and psyllium husk.

4. Spread the batter on a greased baking pan. Add the fried onions and bacon on top.

5. Bake for 20 minutes.

Lunch: *Parmesan Tilapia*

Dinner: *Chicken Casserole*

DAY 38

Breakfast: *Cloud Bread BLT*

Lunch: *Ground Beef Plate*

Serves 2|20 min
Net carbs: 4% (5g/0.18oz) | Fiber: 0.8% (1g/0.03oz) | Fat: 60% (78g/2.7oz)
Protein: 36% (47g/1.66oz) | kcal: 913

INGREDIENTS

- ¾ lb ground beef
- 4 oz shredded cheddar cheese
- 2 oz butter
- 2 oz lettuce
- 2 tbsp olive oil
- ½ green bell pepper
- ½ cucumber
- Salt and pepper

PREPARATION:

1. Cook the ground beef in butter until it gets brown.

2. Lower the heat and add the seasonings.

3. Serve it with cheese and raw vegetables. Add some olive oil as well.

Dinner: *Turkey with Cream-Cheese Sauce*

DAY 39

Breakfast: *Pancakes with Cream and Berries*

Lunch: *Red Pepper, Asparagus & Squash Saute*

Dinner: Tuna Casserole

Serves 4 | 30 min
Net carbs: 3% (5g/0.18oz) | Fiber: 2% (3g/0.1oz) | Fat: 60% (83g/3oz)
Protein: 32% (43g/1.5oz) | kcal: 953

INGREDIENTS

- 15 oz tuna in olive oil
- 6 oz baby spinach
- 5 oz finely chopped celery stalks
- 2 oz butter
- 1 finely chopped yellow onion
- 4 oz shredded parmesan cheese
- 1 finely chopped green bell pepper
- 4 tbsp olive oil
- 1 cup mayonnaise
- 1 tsp chili flakes
- Salt and pepper

PREPARATION:

1. Preheat the oven to 200-degrees Centigrade.

2. Fry onion, bell pepper and celery in butter. Add salt and pepper for seasoning.

3. Combine tuna, mayonnaise, chilli flakes and cheese with the fried veggies in a greased baking dish. Bake it until the color turns golden brown.

4. Serve with olive oil and baby spinach.

DAY 40

Breakfast: *Paleo Bread*

Serves 20 | 1 hour 5 min

Net carbs: 38% (24g/0.85oz) | Fiber: 6% (4g/0.14oz) | Fat: 38% (24g/0.85oz)

Protein: 16% (10g/0.35oz) | kcal: 266

INGREDIENTS

- 6 eggs
- 7 oz pumpkin seeds
- 7 oz almonds
- 4 oz sunflower seeds
- 3 oz sesame seeds
- 3 oz flaxseed
- 2 oz walnuts
- ⅓ cup olive oil
- 1 tbsp crushed fennel seeds
- 2 tsp salt
- ½ tsp white wine vinegar

PREPARATION:

1. Preheat the oven to 150-degrees Centigrade.

2. Combine the dry ingredients. Then slowly add the eggs, oil and vinegar to prepare the dough.

3. Put it on a non-stick bread pan and bake for an hour.

Lunch: *Sauteed Squash with Onions & Tomatoes*

Dinner: *Cajun Sirloin with Mushroom Leek Sauce*

DAY 41

Breakfast: *Eggs and Bacon*

Lunch: *Cobb Salad with Ranch Dressing*

Serves 2 | 20 min |
Net carbs: 4% (7g/0.3oz) | Fiber: 5% (8g/0.3oz) | Fat: 56% (97g/3.4oz)
Protein: 35% (61g/2.15oz) | kcal: 1161

INGREDIENTS

- 5 oz iceberg lettuce
- 3 oz bacon
- 2 oz blue cheese
- 2 boiled, peeled and chopped eggs
- 1 chopped tomato
- 1 chopped avocado
- ½ rotisserie chicken
- 3 tbsp mayonnaise
- 2 tbsp water
- 1 tbsp chives
- 1 tbsp ranch seasoning
- Salt
- Ground black pepper

PREPARATION:

1. Prepare the dressing first with ranch seasoning, mayonnaise, water, salt and pepper.

2. Cut the chicken. Fry the bacon so that it gets crispy.

3. Form a layer of lettuce on the plate. Place the vegetables, chicken, bacon and eggs on it. Season with salt and pepper. Add the dressing and chives before serving.

Dinner: *Shrimp Scampi Spinach Salad*

45 DAYS KETO DIET CHALLENGE

Breakfast: *Mushroom Omelet*

Lunch: *Mixed Spice Burgers*

Dinner: *Asparagus-Mushroom Frittata*

Serves 8|45 min

Net carbs: 18% (4g/0.14oz) | Fiber: 4% (1g/0.03oz) | Fat: 36% (8g/0.3oz)

Protein: 40% (9g/0.3oz) | kcal: 130

INGREDIENTS

- 8 large eggs
- 1 thinly sliced large onion
- 8 oz asparagus spears
- ½ cup whole-milk ricotta cheese
- ½ cup finely chopped sweet green pepper
- ¼ cup sliced baby portobello mushrooms
- 1 tbsp olive oil
- 2 tbsp lemon juice
- ½ tsp pepper
- ½ tsp salt

PREPARATION:

1. Mix eggs, cheese, lemon juice, salt and pepper in a bowl.

2. Cook asparagus, onion, mushrooms and pepper at medium heat until they get tender. Transfer it to the plate

3. Take 8 spears from the cooked asparagus and arrange them on the eggs any way you prefer.

4. Cut rest of the asparagus and add them to the empty skillet with leftover liquid.

5. Bake the egg mixture uncovered until it sets well. Then cut into several wedges and serve.

DAY 43

Breakfast: *Tomato Feta Soup*

Serves 6 | 30 min

Net carbs: 27% (8g/0.3oz) | Fiber: 7% (2g/0.07oz) | Fat: 43% (13g/0.46oz)

Protein: 13% (4g/0.14oz) | kcal: 170

INGREDIENTS

- 30 oz canned peeled tomatoes
- 2 garlic cloves
- 3 cups water
- ¼ cup chopped onion
- ⅔ cup crumbled feta cheese
- ⅓ cup heavy cream
- 1 tbsp tomato paste

- 2 tbsp butter
- 1 tsp pesto sauce
- 1 tsp dried basil
- 1 tsp honey
- ½ tsp salt
- ½ tsp dried oregano
- Pinch of black pepper

PREPARATION:

1. Heat the butter first and then add in the onions. Cook for a couple of minutes.

2. Add garlic to this concoction and keep cooking for one more minute.

3. Mix in pesto, tomatoes, oregano, basil, tomato paste, salt, pepper and water. Let it reach a boiling temperature and then lower the heat for simmering.

4. Add honey and cook for 20 minutes at medium heat.

5. When the tomatoes get soft, blend it to form a smooth consistency.

6. Introduce feta cheese and cream to cook for a minute.

7. Serve warm and fresh.

Lunch: *Cabbage Roll Soup*

Dinner: *Shrimp Scampi Spinach Salad*

Breakfast: *Coconut Porridge*

Lunch: *Grilled Tuna Salad*

Serves 2 | 10 min

Net carbs: 6% (9g/0.3oz) | Fiber: 4% (6g/0.2oz) | Fat: 53% (79g/2.79oz)

Protein: 36% (53g/1.87oz) | kcal: 975

INGREDIENTS

- ¾ lb sliced tuna
- 8 oz green asparagus
- 4 oz leafy greens
- 2 oz cherry tomatoes
- ⅔ cup mayonnaise
- 2 boiled and halved eggs
- ½ thinly sliced red onion
- 2 tbsp pumpkin seeds
- 2 tbsp water
- 1 tbsp olive oil
- 2 tsp garlic pepper
- Salt and pepper

PREPARATION:

1. Prepare the dressing by combining garlic powder, mayonnaise, water, salt and pepper.

2. Cut asparagus lengthwise and fry in butter.

3. Rub the tuna with oil and grill for 5 minutes. Add salt and pepper for seasoning. Slice them after they are done.

4. Bring together the eggs, tomatoes, asparagus, onions and leafy greens on a plate.

5. Spread the tuna on this layer. Top with dressing and some pumpkin seeds.

Dinner: *Chicken and Broccoli with Dill Sauce*

DAY 45

Breakfast: *Smoked Salmon Sandwich*

Lunch: *Creamed Green Cabbage and Chorizo*

Dinner: *Chicken Garam Masala*

Serves 4 | 25 min

Net carbs: 6% (6g/0.2oz) | Fiber: 4% (4g/0.1oz) | Fat: 51% (51g/1.8oz)

Protein: 38% (38g/1.34oz) | kcal: 620

INGREDIENTS

- 25 oz chicken breasts, cut lengthwise
- 1¼ cups coconut cream
- 1 finely chopped red bell pepper
- 3 tbsp butter
- 2½ tbsp sugar-free garam masala
- 1 tbsp finely chopped parsley
- Salt

PREPARATION:

1. Preheat the oven to 200-degrees Centigrade.

2. Fry the chicken pieces in butter at medium high heat.

3. Add half the Garam masala to it.

4. Place the cooked chicken on the baking dish. Sprinkle salt and juices on it.

5. Combine the bell pepper slices, coconut cream and rest of the garam masala mix.

6. Add this mixture to the chicken and bake for 22 minutes.

7. Serve with parsley on top.

Picture: Yaruniv Studios

Sophie Megan Taylor by proxy of:

Rocka Maldini
Roka Maldini
120, Old Railway Track
SVR 9017
Santa Venera
Malta
Malta

malta.publishing@gmail.com

LEGAL NOTICE

jmNXnpFPrL

056484

Printed in Great
Britain
by Amazon